ROCKET SCIENCE
FOR
SMARTYPANTS

Anushka Ravishankar
ILLUSTRATED BY
Pia Alizé Hazarika

DUCKBILL BOOKS

USA | Canada | UK | Ireland | Australia
New Zealand | India | South Africa | China | Singapore

Duckbill Books is part of the Penguin Random House group of companies
whose addresses can be found at global.penguinrandomhouse.com

Published by Penguin Random House India Pvt. Ltd
4th Floor, Capital Tower 1, MG Road,
Gurugram 122 002, Haryana, India

Penguin
Random House
India

First published in Duckbill Books by
Penguin Random House India 2024

ISBN 9780143461067

Typeset in ArcherPro by DiTech Publishing Services Pvt. Ltd
Printed at Thomson Press India Ltd, New Delhi

www.penguin.co.in

ROCKET SCIENCE is the science
used to move a rocket, overcome the pull
of Earth's gravitational field and plot a
course in space.

If you jump down on a trampoline, you move upwards.

This is because every action has an equal and opposite reaction, according to Newton's Third Law of Motion.*

* Newton's Laws of Motion for Smartypants

The same idea is used when a rocket takes off. When **gases** and **smoke** are pushed downwards, the rocket is pushed upwards.

The nose of the rocket usually has a **payload**. Whatever needs to be sent into space goes into the payload. A payload could be a machine to check the weather, or it could contain astronauts!

Below the payload is the **guidance system**. This system has everything needed to take the rocket in the right direction, to keep it from wobbling and so on.

Below the guidance system are the **fuel tanks**. The fuel burns and gives out smoke and gases.

Below the fuel tank are **pumps** and other things that help push these gases downwards and outwards.

THAT'S YOUR FUEL TANK?
BUT I TOLD YOU, YOU WOULD NEED A LOT OF GAS TO TAKE OFF.
NO, THAT'S NOT ENOUGH.

A lot of fuel has to burn to give off a lot of gas. The force of this gas has to be enough to push the rocket upwards, all the way into space. The upward force is called **thrust**.

THRUST

DOWNWARD FORCE OF GAS AND SMOKE

The thrust gets the rocket moving. But Earth's gravity* is still pulling the rocket down.

*Gravity for Smartypants.

For the rocket to escape Earth's gravity, the upward thrust has to be more than the force of gravity pulling the rocket down.

The rocket needs to speed up to about 17,800 miles per hour so that it is not pulled back to the ground by Earth's gravity. That is about a hundred times faster than a superfast train!

The speed that the rocket needs to reach to escape Earth's gravity is called **escape velocity.**

Once the rocket is launched, it will do what it set out to do. This depend on the payload in the nose of the rocket. For example, the payload could be a satellite which has to go around Earth.

Man-made satellites can send messages from one part of Earth to another.

THESE PICTURES ON THE TV ALSO COME FROM A SATELLITE.

NO, THERE ARE NO MICE ON THE SATELLITE!

ONLY THE PICTURES ARE SENT AND RECEIVED THROUGH THE SATELLITE.

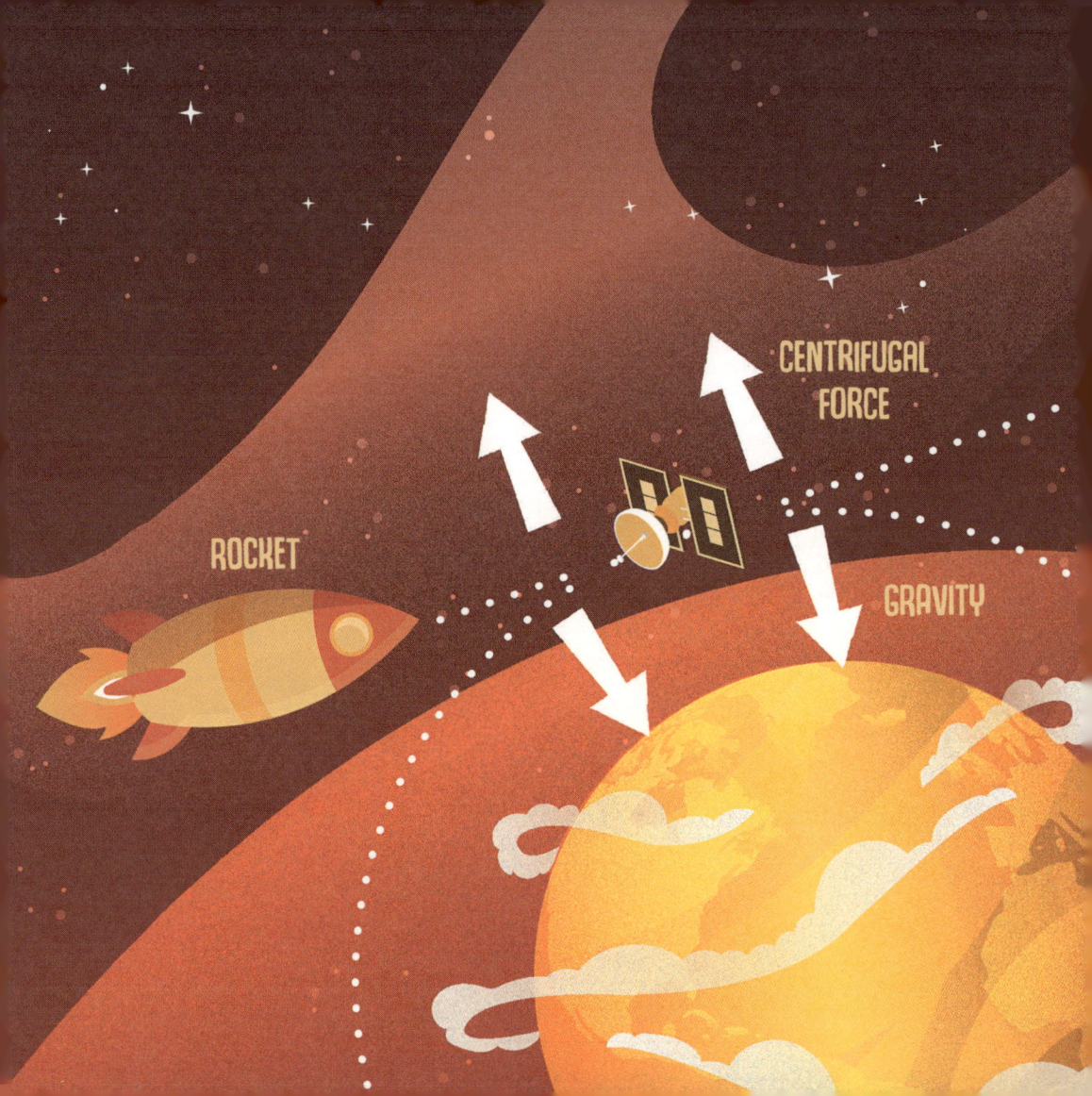

ROCKET

CENTRIFUGAL
FORCE

GRAVITY

The rocket will launch the satellite when it reaches a certain distance from Earth.

There are two forces acting on the satellite. One is the force of gravity that is pulling it towards Earth. The second is **centrifugal force** that is pulling it away from Earth.

The centrifugal force depends on the speed of the satellite.
If the speed is less, the force is less.

If the centrifugal force is less than the force of gravity,
the satellite will fall down to Earth.

CENTRIFUGAL FORCE < GRAVITY

If the centrifugal force is greater than gravity, it will fly off into space.

For the satellite to go around Earth, the centrifugal force has to be equal to gravity.

CENTRIFUGAL FORCE = GRAVITY

CENTRIFUGAL FORCE > GRAVITY

If the satellite is farther away from Earth, it will go slower, because the force of Earth's gravity there will be less.

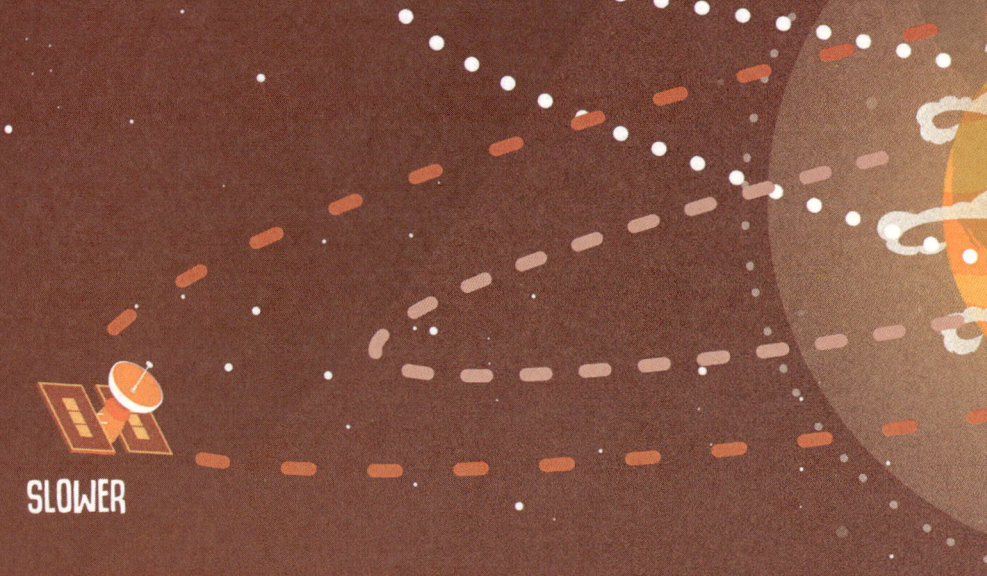

SLOWER

FASTER
YES, IT MUST BE BORING TO GO ROUND AND ROUND.
NO ONE ASKED YOU TO BE A SATELLITE.

If the rocket has to go to the moon, it is launched at a speed that is enough to let it get away from the pull of Earth's gravity. When it gets close to the moon, the moon's gravity pulls it towards the moon while the centrifugal force pulls it away from the moon.

When the two forces are equal, the rocket goes around the moon. To land on the moon, the rocket has to go slower and slower, until the gravity of the moon is greater than the centrifugal force and the rocket is able to land.

Anushka Ravishankar likes science, cats and books, not necessarily in that order. So she decided to write a book to explain science to a cat. The cat doesn't always get the point, but she hopes her readers will.

Pia Alizé Hazarika is an illustrator primarily interested in comics and visual narratives.

Her independent/collaborative work has been published by Penguin Random House India (*The PAO Anthology*), Comix India, Manta Ray Comics, The Pulpocracy, Captain Bijli Comics, Yoda Press, Zubaan Books and the Khoj Artists Collective. She runs PIG Studio, an illustration-driven space, based out of New Delhi.

Her handle on Instagram is @_pigstudio_